100 Key Quotes for GCSE English Literature Revision:

'A Christmas Carol'

By Sarah Hindmarsh

'100 Key Quotes for GCSE English Literature Revision: 'A Christmas Carol" by Sarah Hindmarsh

Copyright © 2019 Sarah Hindmarsh

All rights reserved. No part of this publication may be reproduced, distributed, or transmitted in any form or by any means, including photocopying, recording, or other electronic or mechanical methods, without the prior written permission of the publisher, except in the case of brief quotations embodied in critical reviews and certain other non-commercial uses permitted by copyright law. For permission requests, or to order print copies, contact Creating With Kohla publications using the email address below.

creatingwithkohla@mail.com

First published 2019

Although every precaution has been taken to verify the accuracy of the information contained herein, the author and publisher assume no responsibility for any errors or omissions. No liability is assumed for damages that may result from the use of information contained within.
1) GCSE revision 2) Non-Fiction

Contents

How to use This Book..4

Chapter 1 – A Christmas Carol Stave 1...5

Chapter 2 – A Christmas Carol Stave 2...26

Chapter 3 – A Christmas Carol Stave 3...46

Chapter 4 – A Christmas Carol Stave 4...67

Chapter 5 – A Christmas Carol Stave 5...87

Last Word 107

How to use This Book

The 100 Key Quotes for GCSE English Literature Revision series is designed to be a companion guide to some of the most widely used texts for The GCSE English Literature Exams. It is suitable for use with all exam boards and for all abilities.

This book is not a substitute for reading the full text, however it will highlight some of the most crucial and meaningful quotes from the book, as well as help students write detailed and meaningful analysis of those quote. Students are encouraged to read the full text several times as this is the best way to fully understand the context.

The information contained within will highlight links to the wider themes of the text, links to other quotes in other places in the text, and ways to develop an answer to essay questions and short answer questions. It analyses the literary devices and techniques used and suggests the types of questions each quote might be used to answer.

This book should make revision for English Language GCSEs less onerous and the texts easier to understand.

You can use the book to identify quotes suitable for any revision questions set; and as a basis for learning quotes to put into your exam answers. Whilst all the quotes contained within are useful, not all the useful quotes are contained within! Students may wish to add their own favourites to the list.

Chapter 1 – A Christmas Carol Stave 1

Quote 1

"Scrooge was his sole executor, his sole administrator, his sole assign, his sole residuary legatee, his sole friend and sole mourner."

Techniques:

Repetition of the word 'sole' drives home to the reader how important this quote is.

A *list* is used to evoke a sense of character, it emphasises the isolated nature of his life.

Significance:

This quote shows how isolated Marley had become due to his lifestyle. It is how Scrooge is likely to end up if he does not change his ways.

Related Quote:

"even Scrooge was not so dreadfully cut up"
This reinforces the sense of a man who was alone in the world as even his only friend didn't care very much about his death. It is a warning to the reader not to emulate the mistakes made by Marley.

Bigger picture:

This quote is a comment on the pitfalls of being obsessed with money. It shows that people who live a lifestyle ruled by *greed* and avarice end up alone and miserable. This ties into the theme of *socialism vs capitalism.*

Use this quote in questions about:

Scrooge
Marley
Greed
Socialism vs Capitalism

Quote 2

"a squeezing, wrenching, grasping, scraping, clutching, covetous old sinner"

Techniques:

A *list* of emotive adjectives evokes a sense of Scrooge's character and is designed to put a negative image of him in the mind of the reader.

A *semantic field* of things that are tight or squeezing implies a person who does not part with money easily.

Significance:

This description of Scrooge is one of two opposing descriptions that book-end the novel. This one at the beginning paints a picture of a thoroughly unpleasant person who nobody likes. It is intended to show that people who are obsessed with money and business and don't value human beings more than wealth are to be despised.

Related quotes:

"A frosty rime was on his head, and on his eyebrows and his wiry chin."
This shows further negative aspects of his character with the use of the word 'frosty' to show both the white hair that gives an insight into the age of the character, and the coldness of his personality and temperament.

"No man or woman ever once in all his life inquired the way to such and such a place."
This shows that Scrooge's obsession with money and wealth has made him so unapproachable that other people act almost as though he does not exist. If they acknowledge him at all it is to move out of his way and avoid him.

Bigger picture:

This is related to the theme of *human compassion*. It shows how negatively people see those who don't value human life above money and how wealth and being obsessed with business and making more money can twist people into caricatures of themselves. It also relates to the theme of *greed*.

Use this quote in questions about:

Scrooge
Redemption
Compassion
Greed
Character development
Socialism vs Capitalism

Quote 3

"But he couldn't replenish it for Scrooge kept the coal box in his own room; and so surely as the clerk came in with the shovel, the master predicted that it would be necessary for them to part."

Techniques:

Inference. The fact that Scrooge would fire the clerk for costing him money is not explicitly stated but is so heavily implied that the reader cannot miss it.
This shows a *contrast* with the way Scrooge treats people at the end of the book.

Significance:

This shows how badly Scrooge treats other people at the beginning of the book. It illustrates how his character has come to think people are unimportant.

Related quote:

"The clerk's fire was so very much smaller that it looked like one coal"
This uses *hyperbole* to illustrate the extent to which Scrooge treats others badly.

Bigger picture:

This quote relates to the themes of *greed* and the *capitalism vs socialism*. It shows how those working in organisations that value money above people suffer and have no power to improve their positions.

Use this quote in questions about:

Greed
Capitalism vs Socialism
Scrooge
Poverty
Bob Cratchitt and the Cratchitt family
Redemption
Working conditions/society in Dickensian time

Quote 4

"His face was ruddy and handsome; his eyes sparkled, and his breath smoked again." about Scrooge's nephew

Techniques:

A *list* is used to evoke a sense of the character of Scrooge's nephew.

There is a *contrast* between the words implying warmth applied to Scrooge's nephew and the words implying cold applied to Scrooge himself.

Significance:

This quote shows how positively Scrooge's nephew, who values people and family, and always makes the effort to invite Scrooge to celebrations is viewed by the narrator. This highlights even further how negatively Scrooge is viewed as their descriptions are in direct contrast.

Related Quote:

"a cheerful voice"
This shows that the nephew is a joyful person, that valuing people above money has made him happier than all of Scrooge's wealth has made him.

Bigger picture:

This quote relates to the theme of *family*. Scrooge, who does not value family, is miserable whilst his nephew, who does value family, is happy. This is a clear message to the reader that family is important, and that being with family at Christmas is especially important. It also relates to *capitalism vs socialism* as socialist Fred is described in clear contrast to capitalist Scrooge.

Use this quote in questions about:

Family
Scrooge
Socialism vs Capitalism
Characterisation
Fred

Quote 5

"What right have you to be merry? You're poor enough."

Who said it?
Scrooge to his nephew

Techniques:

Dialogue is used to show the relationship between Scrooge and his nephew. A *rhetorical question* helps the reader to engage with the idea.

Significance:

Scrooge shows here that he values money above everything else and believes that money makes people happy. He implies that those who are poor cannot be happy.

Related quote:

"What reason have you to be morose? You're rich enough."
This shows that Scrooge's nephew has realised that Scrooge is not happy and that money has not bought him happiness. It also shows that the nephew is not afraid of Scrooge like some people as he has the courage to stand up to him. It helps the reader to relate to the nephew.

Bigger Picture:

This quote relates to the theme of *money*. It shows that money cannot buy happiness. Depicting the poor man as being happier than the rich man shows that happiness is a state of mind, not a state of wealth. The nephew is happy because he has a full and rich life with a family he loves. Scrooge is unhappy despite his great wealth because he has isolated himself from the people he should have loved.

Use this quote in questions about:

Poverty/money
Scrooge
Fred
Socialism vs capitalism
Happiness

Quote 6

"There are many things from which I might have derived good, by which I have not profited"

Who said it?
Scrooge's nephew, Fred.

Techniques:

Connotation: the word "good" has different meanings to the two characters. Immediately before this quote Scrooge uses the word to mean money and the nephew in this line refers to the good some things do to the soul, rather than to the bank account.

Foreshadowing: In the final stave the actions that do Scrooge the most good are the ones that involve giving away his money rather than those that involve making more profit.

Significance:

This quote explains in part why Scrooge's nephew continues to invite Scrooge to Christmas dinner every year. Although he knows Scrooge will not come it does his own soul good to be sure to invite him so that he is not guilty of leaving him out.

Related quote:

"though it has never put a scrap of gold or silver in my pocket I believe that is has done me good and will do me good;"

Bigger Picture:

This quote relates to the themes of *money* and *happiness*. It signals to the reader that the author believes that money does not make people happy, but rather that they must seek out happiness in other things.

Use this quote in questions about:

Money
Happiness
Fred

Quote 7

"Portly gentlemen, pleasant to behold,"

Techniques:

Alliteration is used in "portly" and "pleasant" to draw the reader's attention to the importance of the description of the men

Contrast with the unpleasant way Mr Scrooge is described suggests to the reader that these men are to be liked where Mr Scrooge is not.

Significance:

Throughout the first stave we see characters engaged in kind or charitable acts described in a positive way. These men are working for a charity and attempting to generate donations to help the poor at Christmas. The author wants this kind of action to be seen as desirable by the reader and therefore uses positive language to give a good impression of the men.

Related quote:

"His face was ruddy and handsome" said of Mr Scrooge's nephew, Fred, when he first enters the counting house.

Bigger picture:

This quote relates to the theme of *socialism* which the author portrays in a positive light. That he describes men working for a charity in such positive terms indicates to the reader that the author thinks people should be generous to those less fortunate than themselves. He contrasts this with a negative description of the capitalist Mr Scrooge, and even makes the socialist characters happy while the capitalist is miserable.

Use this quote in questions about:

Charity
Socialism vs Capitalism
Redemption
Author's view of a "good man".

Quote 8

"Are there no prisons?"

Who said it?
Scrooge, to the men from the charity

Techniques:

A question is used to help the reader engage with the text. When a reader sees a question they automatically formulate their own answer, this means they have invested in the text emotionally.

Significance:

Scrooge is showing his low opinion of the poor. He believes that they are worthy only of a cell in a debtor's prison, and not of any home comforts. This further emphasises to the reader what an unpleasant person Scrooge is.

Related quote:

"It's enough for a man to understand his own business." This dialogue shows that Scrooge thinks only of himself.

Bigger Picture:

It is not surprising to the reader that Scrooge believes prisons are an acceptable option for the poor given that he spends so little of his vast fortune making himself comfortable. What we know of Scrooge makes it laughable that he would pay to help someone else have comforts in their life when he does not even do that for himself.

At the end of the third stave the spirit throws Scrooge's own words back at him to make him realise how despicable his actions were before the spirits visited him.

Use this quote in questions about:

Scrooge
Redemption
Charity
Poverty
Life in Dickensian times

Quote 9

"If they had rather die," said Scrooge, "they had better do it, and decrease the surplus population."

Techniques:

This *statement* of Scrooge's is designed to *shock* the reader because it shows how little he values human life.

Significance:

This is one of Scrooge's character-defining statements at the beginning of the book. It makes his character appear repellent. It contrasts sharply with the attitude of the men from the charity who believe that everyone deserves a little bit of cheer at Christmas time. Scrooge does not even believe they deserve to live. This shows the high regard in which he holds money - to the extent he believes a man is worthless if he does not have any.

Related quote:

"It is more than usually desirable that we should make some provision for the poor and destitute, who suffer greatly at the present time,"
This quote said by one of the men from the charity provides a *contrast* to Scrooge's views.

Bigger picture:

This quote relates to the themes of *socialism vs capitalism* and *poverty* because it emphasises the gap between rich and poor. The gap is so large the rich do not even see the poor as humans worthy of living. It shows how difficult life was for the poor at the time the text was written, and how dependent they were on the charity of others.
This quote is also repeated back to Scrooge to show him the error of his ways when he enquires about whether Tiny Tim will live.

Use this quote in questions about:

Scrooge
Redemption
Charity
Poverty in Dickensian times

Quote 10

"A poor excuse for picking a man's pocket every twenty-fifth of December."

Who said it?
Scrooge - to his clerk, Bob Cratchitt, who wanted the day off for Christmas.

Techniques:

Metaphor is used to show how Scrooge feels about his staff being able to take a day off for Christmas and still be paid the days wages.

Significance:
This shows that Scrooge does not consider that the wages he pays his clerk are already little better than slave labour, and further emphasises his dislike of Christmas day celebrations.

Related quote:

"Be here all the earlier next morning." - shows that Scrooge still wants his pound of flesh from his clerk even if he has begrudgingly allowed him the entire day off for Christmas.

Bigger picture:

This scene *foreshadows* that Bob Cratchitt will be late on the morning of the 26th and sets up why he appears so fearful when that happens. It relates to the theme of *poverty* showing that the poor had to be grateful and subservient to their rich employers because if they were to lose their pitiful wages it could mean their family starving or being unable to pay rent.

Use this quote in questions about:

Scrooge
Christmas
Poverty
Bob Cratchitt and the Cratchitt family
Redemption
Life in Dickensian times

Quote 11

"Scrooge took his melancholy dinner in his usual melancholy tavern"

Techniques:

Repetition of the word melancholy emphasises how miserable Scrooge's life is before the spirits visit.

Significance:

This quote creates a contrast with the life Scrooge leads after the spirits visit. He is painted as miserable and alone and stuck in his ways.

Related quote:

"Darkness is cheap, and Scrooge liked it."

Bigger picture:

This quote relates to the theme of *happiness* and shows that despite all his money Scrooge has not been able to buy himself happiness or companionship.

Use this quote in questions about:

Scrooge
Happiness
Redemption

Quote 12

"Had a dismal light about it, like a bad lobster in a dark cellar," Said of Marley's ghostly head when it appeared in place of the door knocker.

Techniques:

Simile helps the reader to picture something by using a familiar image to help them.

There is a *semantic field* of darkness in this sentence which has the *connotation* of something dark and frightening still to happen. This *foreshadows* the appearance of the three spirits as well as creating an atmosphere of foreboding at this moment.

Significance:

This is Scrooge's first sighting of Marley's ghost. It sets the tone of the appearance of the spirits as something unpleasant to be endured.

Related quote:

"He *did* pause, with a moment's irresolution, before he shut the door; and he *did* look cautiously behind it at first," The use of *repetition* and *italics* here shows that the usually unflappable and unfanciful Scrooge is indeed unsettled by the appearance of the ghost although he still doubts his own eyes and pretends it did not happen.

Bigger picture:

Each of the spirits was mentioned in the context of light or darkness in some way, for example the light streaming from the head of the first spirit, possibly representing that Scrooge achieved some kind of enlightenment on his journey with them.

Use this quote in questions about:

Marley's ghost
The spirit world
Scrooge's denial of what is happening

Quote 13

"I wear the chain I forged in life,"

Who said it?
Marley's ghost

Techniques:

The use of the *verb* "forged" suggests that great care was taken over the making of the chain.

Dialogue gives the statement immediacy and power

Significance:

Marley's chain is long and ponderous. It is made of all things related to money. This suggests that he is forced to drag around with him the things he found most important in life. Because money and gold are heavy his chain is therefore difficult to bear. It shows that through the way he lived he created his own punishment for the afterlife.

Related quote:

"It was made (for Scrooge observed it closely) of cash-boxes, keys, padlocks, ledgers, deeds and heavy purses wrought in steel."

Bigger picture:

At the time the book was written society was extremely religious. People would therefore have believed overwhelmingly in the afterlife and purgatory. This image of someone creating their own punishment through their actions and values would have had a great impact.

Use this quote in questions about:

Money
Socialism vs capitalism
Scrooge
Marley's ghost
Greed

Quote 14

"What evidence would you have of my reality beyond that of your own senses?"

Who said it?
Marley's ghost

Techniques:

A *rhetorical question* is used here as a technique to persuade that the ghost is real. There is no possible answer to this question, but the spirit asks it all the same, and Scrooge fumbles for an answer, as the reader would also do.

Significance:

This shows how stubborn Scrooge is, and how in denial about anything which does not fit with his world view. If he will not even believe the sight before his eyes then the reader knows that it will be a giant task to change him.

Related quote:

"There's more of gravy than of grave about you," this pun shows that scrooge will make up any explanation for the appearance of the ghost as he is desperate for this experience not to be real.

Bigger picture:

This quote is part of Scrooge's character arc. In order to change the first thing he must do is accept the reality of the ghost. Only then will he be able to accept the spirits and the things they have to show him. Without this acceptance he cannot develop as a person and mend his ways.

Use this quote in questions about:

Scrooge
The spirit world
Superstition
Redemption
Marley's Ghost

Quote 15

"If that spirit goes not forth in life it is condemned to do so after death. It is doomed to wander through the world."

Who said it?
Marley's ghost

Techniques:

There is a *semantic field* of being sentenced or fated present in this quote. The words "condemned" and "doomed" suggest a difficult fate, or punishment for past misdeeds.

Significance:

Marley's ghost has not been able to pass into heaven because he did not do enough with the life he was given. This is the first warning to Scrooge that his fate might be similar to that of the ghost.

Related quote:

The extract continues "and witness what it cannot share, but might have shared on earth and turned to happiness!"

Bigger picture:

This quote relates to the themes of *generosity* and *the importance of fellow-man* suggesting that a life lived alone and without friends to share experiences and riches with those riches are meaningless. It suggests that the feeding of the soul is the most important aspect of life.

Use this quote in questions about:

Scrooge
Charity
Generosity
Redemption
Marley's ghost

Quote 16

"But you were always a good man of business Jacob,"

Who said it?
Scrooge

Techniques:

The phrase "good man of business" *is repeated* several times throughout the first stave. It emphasises the importance of this in Scrooge's esteem at the start of the book.

In this *dialogue* exchange Scrooge's desperation becomes increasingly clear.

Significance:

Scrooge believes that business and making the most of business opportunities and making as much money as possible are the most important facets of a man's character. He does not want to admit that this gives him a narrow and fettered view of the world.

Related quote:

"No space of regret can make amends for one life's opportunities misused!" - Marley informs Scrooge that he did not make good choices in his life because he was too obsessed with making money.

Bigger picture:

This quote relates to the themes of *greed* and *socialism vs capitalism* and shows that Scrooge putting business and money above all other things is a poor way to live life and will ultimately be punished in the afterlife.

Use this quote in questions about:

Scrooge
Greed
Socialism vs Capitalism
Marley's ghost
Redemption

Quote 17

"Mankind was my business. The common welfare was my business; charity, mercy, forbearance and benevolence were all my business."

Who said it?
Marley's ghost

Techniques:

Repetition of the word "business" is used to make the word seem sour. Marley's ghost speaks with contempt of business, and emphasises that the second *connotation* of the word whereby it means "concern or interest" rather than the process of making money is the more important of the two possible meanings.

Significance:

Marley's ghost wishes to emphasise to Scrooge that he should not live his life alone and only for himself. He is trying to tell Scrooge that ignoring the plight of other people when he has the means to help them is wrong.

Related quote:

"We should make some slight provision for the poor and destitute" said by the men from the charity, who are an example of how Marley's ghost is telling Scrooge he should aspire to live.

Bigger picture:

This quote relates to the theme of *socialism vs capitalism* and *generosity* it is an encouragement to charitable actions, and a warning to those who don't undertake such actions.

Use this quote in questions about:

Marley's ghost
Redemption
Socialism vs Capitalism
Charity/generosity
Greed

Quote 18

"I'm here tonight to warn you that you have yet a chance and hope of escaping my fate. A chance and hope of my procuring."

Who said it?
Marley's ghost

Techniques:

The use of the *verb* escaping implies that Scrooge is currently on the path to the same fate at Marley suffered and he must take evasive action if he is not to be bound by the same chain when he dies.

There is a *semantic field* of hopefulness in the *repetition* of "chance and hope" that suggests all is not lost and there is still potential for Scrooge to change.

Significance:

This shows that Marley has been changed by what he has learned in the afterlife and realised that the person who was the closest thing to a friend that he had in life is in danger of suffering for eternity as Marley himself does. That Marley is able to concern himself with Scrooge's fate shows that there is hope that people can be redeemed no matter how grave their sins so far.

Bigger picture:

This quote relates to the theme of *redemption* which would have been a theme that resonated with a lot of people in a highly religious society.

Use this quote in questions about:

Redemption
Scrooge
Marley's Ghost

Quote 19

"The misery with them all was, clearly, that they sought to interfere, for good, in human matters, and had lost the power forever."

Techniques:

This is a *long and complex sentence* which indicates that the suffering of the ghosts visible is never ending.

Significance:

Marley's ghost shows this to Scrooge to shock him. Scrooge now knows without a doubt that there are many people suffering such a fate, and the extent of their misery. This provides incentive for him to cooperate with the spirits and change his ways.

Related quote:

"Many had been personally known to Scrooge in their lives."

Bigger picture:

This quote is related to *redemption* in that it shows that Scrooge must seek redemption whilst he is still alive as it will be too late after he is dead. He will lose the ability to do good, and therefore will not be able to compensate for his lifetime of selfishness and greed.

Use this quote in questions about:

Scrooge
Redemption
The spirit world
Marley's ghost
Socialism vs capitalism
Charity/generosity

Quote 20

"He tried to say 'Humbug!' but stopped at the first syllable"

Techniques:

There is a *contrast* here between how easily the word "humbug" rolled off Scrooge's tongue at the beginning of the stave and the difficulty he has in saying it here.

The *repetition* of the *exclamation* shows that the use of this word is significant to the book, in particular to Scrooge's character arc.

Significance:

This is the first indication we have that Scrooge might actually change as a result of the night's events. That he tries to say humbug and is unable to suggests that he is no longer so confident and certain in his beliefs.

Bigger Picture:

This quote relates to the theme of *redemption*. The reader begins to think that there is hope for the redemption of Scrooge after all.

Use this quote in questions about:

Scrooge/changes in Scrooge
Redemption

Chapter 2 – A Christmas Carol Stave 2

Quote 21

"He could no more go to sleep than go to Heaven,"

Techniques:

Hyperbole is used here. Scrooge is obviously more capable of sleeping than of going to heaven but the dramatic exaggeration adds to the sense of urgency in this passage.

Significance:

This also shows the level of his anticipation about the spirit visits he has been promised, including wondering if they will happen at all. It is a reflection of his state of mind, and how upset he has been by the visit of Marley's ghost and what the ghost told him about his fate.

Related quote:

"Scrooge went to bed again and thought, and thought, and though it over and over and could make nothing of it."

Bigger picture:

This is an oblique reference to the fact that if Scrooge doesn't mend his ways he will not go to Heaven when he dies. It relates to the theme of *redemption.*

Use this quote in questions about:

Building tension
Scrooge/changes in Scrooge
Redemption
The spirit world
How the visits from the Spirits affect Scrooge

Quote 22

"It was a strange figure - Like a child: yet not so much like a child as like an old man."

Techniques:

Simile is used here to enhance the description of the spirit using an image that is familiar to the reader.

An *oxymoron* is also used to show the strangeness of the spirit's appearance. It is not possible for the spirit to be both a child and an old man, this adds to the picture of the spirit as a disturbing and frightening entity.

Significance:

The spirit is described as being something otherworldly and unknowable. This helps the reader to suspend disbelief as they will expect to read about impossible things happening if they sufficiently believe that the spirit is a magical or supernatural entity.

Related quote:

"The strangest thing about it was, that from the crown of its head there sprung a bright, clear jet of light by which all this was visible."

Bigger picture:

In the context of the time this was written the idea of the supernatural would have been unsettling. Fear of God, and therefore fear of his spirits, was common. Readers at the time would need to believe that this spirit was sent from God to help Scrooge achieve redemption, and convincing them it was an otherworldly spirit would therefore have been important.

Use this quote in questions about:

The Ghost of Christmas Past
The spirit world
The spirits as redeeming angels
Redemption

Quote 23

"Would you so soon put out, with worldly hands, the light I give?"

Techniques:

A *rhetorical question* is used here to encourage the reader to think more deeply about Scrooge's request that the spirit cover himself and what the spirit, and the light, represents.

Significance:

This passage shows Scrooge's discomfort with the supernatural and spirituality. It suggests that he, and others, have kept the world in darkness by their actions.

Related quote:

"Is it not enough that you are one of those whose passions made this cap, and force me through whole trains of years to wear it low upon my brow?"

Bigger Picture:

This is a religious reference to the light of the saviour and suggests that Scrooge's sin and obsession with money and greed above all else, to the detriment of his soul, dims that light.

Use this quote in questions about:

The Ghost of Christmas Past
The spirit world
The spirits as redeeming angel
Redemption
Greed

Quote 24

"Your lip is trembling," said the Ghost. "And what is that upon your cheek?"

Who said it?
The Ghost of Christmas past.

Techniques:

The use of the *verb* "trembling" suggests Scrooge is in a vulnerable mental state.

A *rhetorical question* is used to draw attention to Scrooge's face and *infers* that he is crying.

Significance:

This is the first time we see Scrooge as being capable of any real emotion other than fear. The reader can now see that he is more human than he was initially portrayed. This is designed to make the reader want to know what could have moved him to tears and what could have happened to make him so hard and unpleasant as an old man.

Related quote:

"Scrooge muttered, with an unusual catching in his voice, that it was a pimple." - this gives further signs of Scrooge's emotional state and shows that he is having trouble holding himself together.

Bigger picture:

The second stave is used to build the reader's sympathy for Scrooge. This begins with his reaction to seeing his childhood home for the first time in so many years.

Use this quote in questions about:

Scrooge/changes in Scrooge
Redemption
How the visits of the spirits affect Scrooge
How the author builds sympathy for Scrooge

Quote 25

"Why was he filled with gladness when he heard them give each other merry Christmas ... ? What was merry Christmas to Scrooge? Out upon merry Christmas" What good had it ever done to him?"

Techniques:

Many *rhetorical questions* are used here to remind the reader of Scrooge's earlier statements and highlight the *contrast* between his views of Christmas as expressed a few hours earlier and his reaction to hearing merry Christmas here. This is an example of a *textual echo*.

Significance:

This is the first time we see Scrooge's own words repeated back to emphasise how hypocritical his views were at the start of the book. It shows that Scrooge did not always hate Christmas so much and being taken back to his past is reminding him of the fact that it used to bring him joy.

Related quote:

"There was a boy singing a Christmas Carol at my door last night. I should like to have given him something: that's all."

Bigger Picture:

This quote relates to the theme of *Christmas* and shows the joy that it can bring.

Use this quote in questions about:

Scrooge/changes in Scrooge
Christmas
How the visits of the spirits affect Scrooge
Redemption
How the author builds sympathy for Scrooge
The Ghost of Christmas past

Quote 26

"He said, in pity for his former self, 'Poor boy!'"

Who said it?
Scrooge.

Techniques:

Dialogue is used to show Scrooge's emotions at this point.

The *abstract noun* "pity" shows that Scrooge empathises with the boy, and shows us what a tragic childhood Scrooge has that he feels sorry for the child he used to be.

Significance:

This scene helps us to begin to understand why Scrooge finds Christmas a difficult time of the year. He was left alone at school over the Christmas holidays which is a miserable thing for a child to experience. The reader feels as sorry for the boy as Scrooge does.

Related quote:

"A lonely boy was reading by a feeble fire." Scrooge is described as lonely as a boy, and this has continued into his adulthood.

Bigger Picture:

This quote relates to the theme of *family* because it highlights that Scrooge missed out on a loving family as a child and goes some way to explaining why he does not value family as a grown man. It also relates to the theme of *Christmas* as it shows how Scrooge used to spend his Christmases as a child.

Use this quote in questions about:

Christmas
Family
Scrooge's childhood
How the author builds sympathy for Scrooge

Quote 27

"Scrooge's former self grew larger at the words, and the room became a little darker and more dirty."

Techniques:

The words "darker" and "more dirty" are used as a *comparison* to show how Scrooge's school, and concurrently his childhood, deteriorated as he got older.

Significance:

This emphasises how bad Scrooge's childhood was. The reader builds sympathy for him being left for years in a school that was gradually falling down around him.

Related quote:

"There he was, alone again, when all the other boys had gone home for the jolly holidays.

Bigger picture:

The deterioration in the school is echoed in the deterioration in Scrooge's mental state over the years. As the school becomes darker so does Scrooge's heart. This contributes to the hard and unkind person he became when he grew up.

Use this quote in questions about:

Scrooge's childhood
How the writer builds sympathy for Scrooge
Scrooge
The Ghost of Christmas past

Quote 28

"'I have come to bring you home dear brother!' said the child, clapping her tiny hands, and bending down to laugh. 'To bring you home, home, home!'"

Who said it?
Fan, Scrooge's little sister.

Techniques:

The *repetition* of the word home combined with the *gleeful tone* of the *dialogue* gives the impression that this was a positive moment. It shows the importance of the idea of home to Scrooge.

Significance:

Scrooge is collected from the boarding school by his sister. We see in this scene that at one time there was someone whom Scrooge loved and who loved him in return.

Related quotes:

"Father is so much kinder than he used to be that home's like Heaven." This quote shows how unpleasant some parts of Scrooge's childhood were.

"We're to be together all the Christmas long and have the merriest time in all the world."

Bigger Picture:

Although in this scene we see that Scrooge and his little sister were close we learn not long after that she died reasonably young. This could also help to explain why Scrooge is so miserable as an old man, the one person he feels ever truly loved him is gone.

Use this quote in questions about:

Christmas
Scrooge's childhood
Family

Quote 29

"True," said the Ghost. "Your nephew!"
Scrooge seemed uneasy in his mind; and answered briefly, "Yes."

Techniques:

Short sentences are used to emphasise Scrooge's discomfort with the Ghost's statement.

There is an *accusatory tone* to the *dialogue* as if the Ghost is deliberately trying to make Scrooge uncomfortable.

Significance:

This quote shows that Scrooge is beginning to regret the treatment of his nephew. He is reminded that Fred was Fan's son and is therefore the only living reminder of her that he has left. There is an implication that he feels guilty for not making more effort with the son of the person who loved him most in the world.

Related quote:

"Always a delicate creature, whom a breath might have withered." This shows the fragility of Fan's health and therefore Scrooge's happiness.

Bigger Picture:

This quote relates to the theme of *family* and shows Scrooge beginning to realise the value of family. It illustrates how important the spirits believe family is in a person's life.

Use this quote in questions about:

Family
Scrooge's childhood
How the writer builds sympathy for Scrooge
Happiness
The Ghost of Christmas past

Quote 30

"In the hall appeared the schoolmaster himself, who glared at Scrooge with a ferocious condescension, and threw him into a dreadful state of mind by shaking hands with him."

Techniques:

There is a *semantic field* of aggression in describing the schoolmaster, which suggests he had an unpleasant attitude towards his students.

Significance:

This interaction with the schoolmaster suggests that Scrooge lived much of his childhood in fear of the schoolmaster. His apprehension when the schoolmaster shakes hands with him tells the reader that he did not expect this.

Related quote:

"A terrible voice ..." further describes the schoolmaster and shows how his students feared him.

Bigger picture:

We learn in this scene that whilst growing up all the male role models in Scrooge's childhood were hard and unfeeling men who inspired more fear in him than love. This is likely to have resulted in emotional neglect and had a significant impact on how he became as an adult.

Use this quote in questions about:

Scrooge's childhood
How the writer builds sympathy for Scrooge
Life in Dickensian times
The Ghost of Christmas past

Quote 31

"Why, it's old Fezziwig! Bless his heart, it's Fezziwig alive again!"

Who said it?
Scrooge

Techniques:

An *exclamation* is used to show Scrooge's surprise at seeing Fezziwig

Short sentences help to create an atmosphere of astonishment.

Significance:

The upbeat tone of this dialogue shows Scrooge's fondness for old Fezziwig.

Related quote:

Fezziwig "Laughed all over himself from his shoes to his organ of benevolence."

Bigger Picture:

Fezziwig was Scrooge's boss. He was a wealthy man but he was not like Scrooge, he was beloved by his employees and others. He is used as an example of how money does not have to corrupt a person if they do not become obsessed with it.

Use this quote in questions about:

Scrooge's past
Capitalism vs Socialism
Generosity
The Ghost of Christmas past

Quote 32

"The warehouse was as snug, and warm, and dry, and bright a ball-room as you would desire to see upon a winter's night."

Techniques:

A *list* of *adjectives* is used with a *semantic field* of cosiness and pleasantness. This draws the reader's attention to how nice the warehouse appeared, suggesting this was important.

There is a stark *contrast* between Fezziwig's warehouse and Scrooge's counting house.

Significance:

The warehouse is a place of work but it has been transformed for Christmas into a place where people would want to be.

Related quote:

"There was nothing they wouldn't have cleared away, or couldn't have cleared away with old Fezziwig looking on." Shows their fondness for their employer and their excitement for the Christmas celebrations.

Bigger picture:

This quote relates to the theme of *Christmas* and illustrates the difference it can make to a place when those within are happy and generous.

Use this quote in questions about:

Scrooge's past
Christmas
Generosity
Happiness
The Ghost of Christmas Past

Quote 33

"In they all came any how and every how."

Techniques:

The use of the *quantifier* "all" shows that everyone was welcome.

Repetition of the word "how" draws attention to the importance of the fact that everyone was welcomed at Fezziwig's.

Significance:

This quote shows that everyone was welcome at Fezziwig's, and that everyone wanted to be there too. It illustrates that communities can come together at Christmas, and social background and wealth are unimportant in this.

Related quote:

"In came the boy from over the way, who was suspected of not having board enough from his master, trying to hide behind the girl from next door but one." This shows that nobody was turned away - even those who were not explicitly invited - because Fezziwig had the true spirit of Christmas.

Bigger Picture:

This quote relates to the themes of *Christmas* and *generosity* it shows Fezziwig's benevolence and how he values the spirit of Christmas and making people happy. He does not turn anyone away and everyone is keen to come. This is in direct contrast to the way Scrooge is viewed. The descriptions of him in the first stave make it seem unlikely that anyone would want to be around him.

Use this quote in questions about:

The Ghost of Christmas Past
Christmas
Generosity
Happiness

Quote 34

"There were more dance, and there were forfeits, and more dances, and there was cake, and there was a great piece of cold roast ..."

Techniques:

A *list* of all the good things at the party is used to emphasise Fezziwig's generosity.

A *long sentence* is used to suggest there was no end to the good things and good cheer at the party.

Significance:

Fezziwig's party is made to seem to be something that everyone looks forward to all the year long, and which nobody wants to end because Fezziwig is so generous with the use of the warehouse and the food and the entertainment. The list of good things helps to add to the positive atmosphere of celebration at the party.

Bigger Picture:

This quote relates to the theme of *generosity* and helps to explain why Fezziwig was held in such high esteem. This is one of Scrooge's happiest memories. The spirit has shown him this scene to help him remember a time when Christmas made him happy and he was delighted to keep it. It also helps to show him that generosity is a virtue and not a foolish waste of money.

Use this quote in questions about:

Christmas
Generosity
The Ghost of Christmas Past
Dickens' idea of a "good man"

Quote 35

"The happiness he gives is quite as great as if it cost a fortune."

Who said it?
Scrooge

Techniques:

A *simile* is used to compare the effects of spending a small amount of money to a large amount in making people happy.

The use of the *adjective* "great" suggests that the thing Fezziwig has done is important and worthy of praise.

Significance:

Scrooge is realising that it does not cost much to make people happy and that a few small things can make a large difference in the lives of ordinary people. He shows that he understands that Fezziwig was doing a good thing and admires him for it.

Related quotes:

"He has the power to render us happy or unhappy;"

"I should like to be able to say a word or two to my clerk just now."

Bigger picture:

This quote relates to the theme of *generosity*. It is an important point in Scrooge's character arc that he begins to realise that it is not just other people he can make happy through generosity but himself as well. He has seen how happy Fezziwig was at the party and how he used his power over his employees for good, and not to make them miserable. He begins to regret how he has treated his own employee.

Use this quote in questions about:

Christmas
Generosity
How the visit of the spirits affect Scrooge

Quote 36

"There was an eager, greedy, restless motion in the eyes, which showed the passion that had taken root and where the shadow of the growing tree would fall."

Techniques:

A *list* of *adjectives* is used to emphasise the change in Scrooge in this scene in *comparison* to the previous vision of Fezziwig's party.

A *metaphor* is used to describe Scrooge's obsession with money as a tree blocking out the light, as it has blocked out the light from his soul, casting darkness and cold onto him.

Significance:

This is the first time we see signs of avarice in the young Scrooge. This description mirrors the description at the beginning of the first stave with its list of adjectives suggesting greed. This is the first sign from Scrooge's past of his downfall.

Related quote:

"His face had not the harsh and rigid lines of later years; but it had begun to wear the signs of care and avarice."

Significance:

This quote relates to the theme of *greed.* This is the start of the scene in which Scrooge's greed first begins to cause him pain. It shows that people who give in to greed are unhappy through the use of words such as "restless" and "shadow" which have *negative connotations*.

Use this quote in questions relating to:

Greed
Money
Scrooge
The Ghost of Christmas Past

Quote 37

"Another idol has displaced me. ... A golden one"

Who said it?
Scrooge's former girlfriend Belle

Techniques:

The *connotations* of the word "golden" suggest money. The suggestion that Scrooge worships money is a *hyperbole.*

Significance:

This shows how obsessed Scrooge became with money. Even his girlfriend felt that he cared more for money than he did for her. This quote implies that she felt unimportant in Scrooge's life because she did not bring him riches and that was all he wanted.

Related quote:

"I have seen your nobler aspirations fall off one by one, until the master passion, Gain, engrosses you."

Bigger picture:

This quote relates to the theme of *greed* and shows that throughout his adulthood Scrooge has been unable to maintain meaningful relationships with people because he cannot think about anything but money. It reminds us that his longest standing association was with Jacob Marley, who was similarly obsessed with money and their partnership was one of business only, with neither caring much about the other as a person and Scrooge even carrying out business deals at Marley's funeral.

Use this quote in questions relating to:

Greed
Money
Family
Scrooge
The Ghost of Christmas Past

Quote 38

"Tell me, would you seek me out and try to win me now? Ah no!"

Who said it?
Belle

Techniques:

A *rhetorical question* is used to help the reader to understand that Belle already knows Scrooge's nature and make them think about what they know about Scrooge as a person.

Significance:

This quote suggests that Scrooge would not have been interested in Belle had he not met her when they were both poor. Once he became rich he would only have been interested in girls that would constitute a "good marriage" in terms of dowry and social status.

Related quote:

"Can even I believe that you would choose a dowerless girl?"

"Repentance and regret would surely follow,"

Bigger picture:

This scene helps the reader to understand why Scrooge was alone all his life and never married. It suggests that no woman could ever have been good enough because no woman would have had a sufficient dowry or inheritance to make her keep worth his while.

Use this quote in questions about:

Greed
Money
Family
Scrooge
The Ghost of Christmas Past
Life in Dickensian times

Quote 39

"When he thought that such another creature, quite as graceful and full of promise, might have called him father ... his sight grew very dim indeed."

Techniques:

The *implication* of Scrooge's sight growing dim is that he was overcome with tears and could not see through them.

The *abstract noun* "promise" suggests something that might have been and in the *context* of the scene *implies* regret.

Significance:

This scene shows what Scrooge's life might have been like if he had not become obsessed with money and had married Belle. It is a glimpse of the happiness he could have had and a reminder of the misery he brought upon himself.

Related quote:

"His partner lies upon the point of death, I hear; and there he sat alone. Quite alone in the world, I do believe."

Bigger picture:

This quote relates to the theme of *family* and shows the impact of the riches of the soul Scrooge gave up when he chose gold and jewels over family and love.

Use this quote in questions about:

Greed
How the visits of the spirits affect Scrooge
Family
Scrooge
The Ghost of Christmas Past

Quote 40

"Though Scrooge pressed it down with all his force he could not hide the light."

Techniques:

The *phrase* "all his force" suggests Scrooge's desperation to be free of the spirit and the visions of the life he could have had.

The light is a *metaphor* for Scrooge's realisation of the mistakes he has made in his life.

Significance:

Scrooge has now realised that he should not have allowed money to rule his life and that he needs to mend his way and he cannot bear it. He tries to extinguish the light cast by the spirit so that he can be left alone in darkness again but finds this impossible. This shows that he cannot unlearn what he has learned and his enlightenment cannot be undone.

Related quote:

"Scrooge observed that its light was burning high and bright; and dimly connecting that with its influence over him, he seized the extinguisher cap.

Bigger picture:

This quote relates to the theme of *redemption* and Scrooge is trying to resist the changes that he must undertake in himself to achieve this redemption. It shows that he cannot ignore the consequences of his behaviour any longer.

Use this quote in questions about:

How the visits of the spirits affect Scrooge
Redemption
Scrooge
The Ghost of Christmas Past

Chapter 3 – A Christmas Carol Stave 3

Quote 41

"I don't mind calling on you to believe that he was ready for a good broad field of strange appearances and that nothing between a baby and rhinoceros would have astonished him very much."

Techniques:

In this quote the narrator speaks directly to the reader as though the narrator is another character. This was a common technique to appear as though the narrator was in conversation with the reader and therefore draw the reader into the text used in the 19th and early 20th century. It fell out of favour in the latter half of the 20th century and is rarely used now, even when the narration is in first person.

Significance:

This quote shows that Scrooge is becoming more open minded. When he first encountered Marley's ghost he was reluctant to believe that it was real whereas he has now become accustomed to the fact that anything could happen and be made real to him.

Related quotes:

"Being prepared for almost anything, he was not by any means prepared for nothing."

"He wished to challenge the Spirit on the moment of its appearance and did not wish to be taken by surprise and made nervous."

Bigger picture:

Scrooge's entire character is seen to change throughout the book, and his acceptance of the validity and variety of the supernatural world is a part of this. The spirits are later revealed to be of a Godly nature and this shows that Scrooge is becoming more open to religious ideas - in particular he later embraces the idea of Christian charity. This would have been a key part of the transformation of any sinner in the context of the time the book was written.

This quote therefore relates to the theme of *redemption*.

Use this quote in questions about:

Redemption
Scrooge
How the visits of the spirits affect Scrooge
The spirit world

Quote 42

"All this time he lay upon his bed, the very core and centre of a blaze of ruddy light,"

Techniques:

A *semantic field* meaning central is used here to denote that Scrooge is at the middle of the phenomenon, and it is occurring because of him.

Significance:

This quote links the second spirit with light, as they are all three linked to the light of God and the Christian saviour Jesus Christ, who was often described as being The Light.
This quote further establishes how strange and otherworldly the Spirit's visits are.

Related quote:

"More alarming than a dozen ghosts."

"He began to think the source and secrecy of this ghostly light might be in the adjoining room."

Bigger Picture:

This quote relates to the theme of *religion*. **Use this quote in questions about:**

Use this quote in questions about:

Religion
The Ghost of Christmas Present
The spirit world

Quote 43

"In easy state upon this couch there sat a jolly giant, glorious to see."

Techniques:

Consonance is used in the phrase "jolly giant" to emphasise the nature of the Spirit's appearance.

The use of the *adjective* "glorious" tells us the giant was pleasant to look at but also has *connotations* which suggest a link to God.

Significance:

The second spirit is differentiated from that of the first by his pleasant and jolly appearance. He is described in a way designed to put the reader in mind of Santa Claus. This Spirit is not intended to be frightening at first.

Related quote:

"The Spirit's eyes were clear and kind"

"It was clothed in one simple deep green robe, or mantle, bordered with white fur."

Bigger Picture:

This spirit represents all that Christmas should be, and this quote relates to the theme of *Christmas*. It makes sense that the spirit of Christmas Present should be something pleasant and not frightening as the other two spirits are.

Use this quote in questions about:

Religion
The Ghost of Christmas Present
The spirit world
Christmas

Quote 44

"There was nothing very cheerful in the climate or the town, and yet there was an air of cheerfulness abroad."

Techniques:

The *repetition* of the word cheerful shows that it is important that the atmosphere is positive. The *implication* is that the cheerfulness is of the making of the fact that it is Christmas. The word cheerful also has a *connotation* relating to Christmas as it puts the reader in mind of the phrase "Christmas cheer".

Significance:

This quote shows how most people see Christmas, and that it is a time to be happy and rejoice, even though it is cold and the weather is miserable. It shows how ordinary people come together at Christmas time and make a positive atmosphere.

Related quotes:

"The people made a rough, but brisk and not unpleasant kind of music,"

"Blazing away to their dear heart's content" - uses *personification* to describe the chimneys, suggesting that even the buildings were in the Christmas spirit.

Bigger Picture:

This scene is the start of the Spirit showing Scrooge how Christmas is kept by ordinary people, and that poverty and hardship are no barrier to someone having Christmas spirit. It relates to the theme of *Christmas*.

Use this quote in questions about:

The Ghost of Christmas Present
Christmas
Happiness

Quote 45

"He shed a few drops of water on them from it, and their good humour was restored directly."

Techniques:

The *adverb* directly shows that the effect of the water from the Spirit's torch was immediate upon the people.

Significance:

This quote is from the scene describing the spirit sprinkling incense on the people passing by himself and Scrooge. It is implied that this adds to their joys and aids in their keeping good spirits over the festive period.

Related quotes:

"It was a very uncommon kind of torch"

"Would it apply to any kind of dinner on this day?" Asked Scrooge. "To any kindly given and to a poor one most."

Bigger picture:

This quote relates to the theme of *Christmas* and shows how the Spirit wished everyone to keep a merry Christmas. The related quote also related to the themes of *charity* and *generosity* recognising that the poor are those most in need at any time of year, and Christmas most of all.

Use this quote in questions about:

Religion
The Ghost of Christmas Present
The spirit world
Christmas
Charity
Generosity

Quote 46

"'There are some upon this earth of yours,' returned the Spirit, 'Who lay claim to know us, and who do their deeds of passion, pride, ill-will, hatred, envy, bigotry and selfishness in our name, who are as strange to us, and all our kith and kin, as if they had never lived.'"

Techniques:

A *list* of sins is used to show the Spirit's anger and indignation at being linked to those who do bad things in the name of God.

A *simile* is used to help the reader envisage the extent of the difference between the people who commit these sins and those truly following God's word. *Emotive language* is used to show the strength of the author's feelings on this subject and help to persuade the reader to his point of view.

Significance:

The spirit is warning Scrooge not to allow the actions of other people to influence his own, especially when it comes to knowing God and being a good Christian.

Related quote:

"You would deprive them of their means of dining every seventh day."

Bigger picture:

This quote relates strongly to the theme of *religion* and explores the premise that not everybody who claims to be acting in God's name is really doing so.

Use this quote in questions about:

Religion
The Ghost of Christmas Present
Charity
Generosity

Quote 47

"He pocketed on Saturdays but fifteen copies of his Christian name and yet the Ghost of Christmas Present blessed his four-roomed house!"

Techniques:

An *exclamation* is used to illustrate that Scrooge would not have expected this.

There is a *pun* on the colloquial word for shilling and Bob Cratchett's Christian name.

Significance:

This action shows Scrooge that the poor are worthy and deserving of help in the eyes of the Ghost of Christmas Present. It illustrates to him the error of his ways in not helping the poor when the men from the charity asked for donations.

Related quote:

"It was his own kind, generous, hearty nature, and his sympathy with all poor men, that led him straight to Scrooge's Clerk's."

Bigger Picture:

This quote relates to the themes of *generosity* and *socialism*.

Use this quote in questions about:

Religion
The Ghost of Christmas Present
Charity
Generosity
How the visits of the spirits affect Scrooge
The Cratchitt Family

Quote 48

"Alas for Tiny Tim, he bore a little crutch, and had his limbs supported by an iron frame."

Techniques:

The *emotive declaration* "Alas" is used to evoke pity in the reader for Tiny Tim.

The *semantic field* of smallness used in the words to describe Tim emphasises his vulnerability and helplessness.

Significance:

Scrooge is introduced to the sick child for the first time. Language is used to show how Scrooge's sympathies have changed since we first met him. He would not have cared much about Tiny Tim before the Ghosts' visits.

Related quote:

"He hoped that people saw him in the church because he was a cripple, and it might be pleasant to them to remember upon Christmas-day who made lame beggars walk and blind men see."

Bigger picture:

This quote relates to the theme of *family*. It also relates to the theme of *poverty* as it illustrates that poor people did not have access to good health care.

Use this quote in questions about:

Tiny Tim
The Cratchitt family
Family
Poverty
Life in Dickensian times

Quote 49

"Such a bustle ensued that you might have thought a goose the rarest of all birds;"

Techniques:

A *superlative* is used in "rarest" to show how powerful the spirit of festivity was

Hyperbole is also used in describing the actions and delight of the young Cratchitts to emphasise their joy in their Christmas dinner and family celebration.

Significance:

The Cratchitts have very little, but we see here that what they do have they are most thankful for and make the best of. They do not allow their poverty to come between them and a wonderful Christmas.

Related quotes:

"What reason have you to be merry? You're poor enough."

"Tiny Tim, excited by the two young Cratchitts, beat on the table with the handle of his knife, and feebly cried Hurrah!"

Bigger Picture:

Scrooge would have been surprised to see that such a poor family could be so happy and content with their lot, especially at Christmas.
This quote relates to the themes of *poverty* and *family*.

Use this quote in questions about:

The Cratchitt family
Family
Poverty
Life in Dickensian times

Quote 50

"'I see a vacant seat,' replied the Ghost, 'in the poor chimney corner and a crutch without an owner, carefully preserved.'"

Techniques:

The use of the *adverb* "carefully" shows the love which Tiny Tim's family feel for him.

The *imagery* of the vacant seat is designed to evoke emotion, and suggests a hole in the family circle.

Significance:

Scrooge has asked if Tiny Tim will die. These images of the family without him show that he will die. Scrooge shows significant character development in caring about such things. This is a contrast to his declaration that the poor dying would merely reduce the surplus population.

Related quotes:

"Bob held his withered little hand in his, as if he loved the child, and wished to keep him by his side and dreaded that he might be taken from him."

"If these shadows remain unaltered by the Future, the child will die."

Bigger Picture:

This quote relates to the themes of *family* and *poverty*. Tiny Tim would not be in danger of dying if his family could afford to pay for expensive medical treatment. His death would have a major impact on the family.

Use this quote in questions about:

The Cratchitt family
Family
Poverty
How the visits of the spirits affect Scrooge

Quote 51

"'No, no,' said Scrooge. 'Oh no, kind Spirit! Say he will be spared!"

Techniques:

The *repetition* of the word "no" emphasises Scrooge's distress at the idea that Tiny Tim will die. The *exclamation* and *pleading tone* of his cries further demonstrates this.

Significance:

Scrooge is distressed by Tiny Tim's plight as he has not been concerned for anyone in the recent past. This is a moment of realisation for him that there are some things in life that are more complex than men minding their own business and more important than making money. His emotion is genuine.

Related quotes:

"If these shadows remain unaltered by the Future, none other of my race' returned the Ghost, "will find him here."

Bigger picture:

This quote relates to Scrooge's character arc and, most importantly, his *redemption*. The reader can see he is no longer the heartless and unfeeling man he once was. He has demonstrated genuine care for another human being.

Use this quote in questions about:

Tiny Tim
The Cratchitt family
Scrooge
How the visits of the spirits affect Scrooge
The Ghost of Christmas Present

Quote 52

"'What then? If he be like to die, he had better do it, and decrease the surplus population.' Scrooge hung his head to hear his own words quoted by the spirit, and was overcome with penitence and grief."

Techniques:

A *rhetorical question* is used as an *emotive device* to shock the reader and make Scrooge feel guilty.
This is a *literary echo* where Scrooge's own words are repeated back to him to highlight his wrongdoing and make him ashamed.

Significance:

Scrooge was unfeeling enough to suggest in stave one that the poor should simply die if they cannot afford to feed themselves and it would be no great loss. This scene illustrates that the cost of a death is more than the sum of the coins in the victim's pocket. Tiny Tim puts a face, and an innocent face at that, to the masses that Scrooge previously felt no sympathy for and could see no value in. his views are now changed.

Related quote:

"Forbear that wicked cant until you have discovered What the surplus is, and Where it is."

"Will you decide what men shall live and what men shall die?"

Bigger Picture:

This quote relates to the themes of *poverty* and *redemption*. It also relates to the theme of *socialism vs capitalism* as it illustrates that a person's wealth is not the sum of their worth.

Use this quote in questions about:

Redemption
Socialism vs Capitalism
Scrooge
How the visits of the spirits affect Scrooge
The Ghost of Christmas Present

Quote 53

"It should be Christmas-day, I am sure," said she, "on which one drinks the health of such an odious, stingy, hard, unfeeling man as Mr Scrooge."

Techniques:

A *list* of *emotive adjectives* is used to show the strength of Mrs Cratchitt's feelings about Scrooge.

Sarcasm is used to show how ridiculous Mrs Cratchitt feels drinking a toast to Mr Scrooge is.

Significance:

Scrooge is now discovering how other people in his world view him. Mrs Cratchitt is angry that Bob would suggest drinking a toast to Mr Scrooge when his mean-ness is one of the causes of their poverty and of Mr Cratchitt's misery at work.

Related quote:

"I'll drink his health for your sake and the day's," said Mrs Cratchitt, "not for his."

Bigger Picture:

This exchange foreshadows the events of the fourth stave in which people are glad to see Mr Scrooge dead and nobody has a good word to say about him. It relates to the themes of *Christmas* and *Poverty*.

Use this quote in questions about:

Redemption
Socialism vs Capitalism
Scrooge
The Cratchitt Family

Quote 54

"'What place is this?' asked Scrooge. 'A place where miners live, who labour in the bowels of the earth,' returned the Spirit. 'But they know me. See!'"

Techniques:

Personification is used in reference to the earth, "bowels" suggests an ability to eat and digest.

An *exclamation* is used to illustrate the seeming unlikeliness that men who spend their time below ground in such hard labour should carry the spirit of Christmas in their hearts.

Significance:

The spirit is showing Scrooge that all people are able to carry the spirit of Christmas in their hearts, no matter what their circumstances, and that difficulties are no indicator of unhappiness and lack of cheer.

Related quote:

"Even here the two men who watched the light had made a fire that through the loophole in the thick stone wall shed out a ray of brightness"

"Every man among them hummed a Christmas tune, or had a Christmas thought."

Bigger picture:

This quote relates to the theme of *Christmas*.

Use this quote in questions about:

Christmas
The Ghost of Christmas Present
Religion

Quote 55

"While there is infection in disease and sorrow, there is nothing in the world so irresistibly contagious as laughter."

Techniques:

Two polar opposites are *juxtaposed* here to emphasise the ease with which laughter spreads in *comparison* to unpleasant things.

The *implication* is that it is easier to spread good in the world than bad.

Significance:

This shows how dismal Scrooge used to be that he was not affected positively by his nephew's laughter and good nature. It also illustrates how much effort he had to expend to continue to make people miserable.

Related quotes:

"If you should happen to know a man more blessed in a laugh than Scrooge's nephew. all I can say is, I should like to know him too."

"[She] laughed as heartily as he. And their assembled friends, being not a bit behindhand, roared out lustily."

Bigger picture:

This is a *moral message* to the reader that it takes less effort and does more good to pass on good cheer than it does to make someone miserable.

Use this quote in questions about:

Christmas
The Ghost of Christmas Present
Religion
Happiness

Quote 56

"His wealth is of no use to him. He don't do any good with it. He don't make himself comfortable with it."

Who said it?
Scrooge's nephew, Fred.

Techniques:

The *repetition* of the phrase "he don't" emphasises the point the nephew is making.

Fred is using *persuasive* techniques upon his audience by *stating opinion as if it is fact.*

Significance:

Scrooge is shown this scene to help him understand that his wealth is not something others envy, far from it. They pity him because pursuing riches above all else has left him lonely and miserable, and he doesn't even afford himself the comforts he could purchase to make his life easier and more comfortable.

Related quote:

"Who suffers by his ill whims? Himself always."

Bigger picture:

This quote relates to the theme of *greed.*

Use this quote in questions about:

Scrooge
Greed
Christmas
Family
Happiness

62

Quote 57

"Who suffers by his ill whims? Himself always."

Who said it?
Scrooge's nephew Fred

Techniques:

A *rhetorical question* is used to prompt the reader to think more deeply about the consequences of Scrooge's actions.

Short sentences give power and drama to the statements.

Significance:

Scrooge's nephew knows that it doesn't make his Christmas any less merry if Scrooge is not there, and the only person who suffers is Scrooge - alone and miserable on Christmas day. Scrooge has been causing his own misery in his stubbornness.

Related quote:

"He loses some pleasant moments which could do him no harm."

Bigger picture:

This quote relates to the theme of *happiness* and explains why Scrooge is so unhappy while his nephew is so happy. They each choose their outlook on life, and therefore each reap the rewards they sow.

Use this quote in questions about:

Scrooge
Fred
Christmas
Family
Happiness

Quote 58

"From the foldings of its robe it brought two children; wretched, abject, frightful, hideous, miserable."

Techniques:

A *list* of *emotive adjectives* is used to cultivate horror in the reader at the state of the children.

There is a *semantic field* of being scared and unhappy, suggesting this was an important feature of the children.

Significance:

Scrooge looks at the worst sins of mankind in looking at the children. He sees the horror his own actions have wrought upon the world.

Related quote:

"Is it a foot or a claw?"

"They were a boy and a girl. Yellow, meagre, ragged, scowling, wolfish; but prostrate too in their humility."

"Where graceful youth should have filled their features out, and touched them with its freshest tints, a stale and shrivelled hand, like that of age, had pinched, and twisted them,"

Bigger Picture:

This quote relates to the theme of *greed* and shows how mankind has fallen from grace with their obsession with money and riches. For this reason it also relates to the themes of *socialism vs capitalism* and *poverty*.

Use this quote in questions about:

Scrooge
Poverty
Socialism vs capitalism
Greed

Quote 59

"This boy is Ignorance. This girl is Want. Beware of them both ... but most of all beware this boy, for on his brow I see written that which is doom."

Techniques:

The *short sentences* add a dramatic *tone* to the scene.

There are two examples of *repetition* in the phrasing of the introductions of the children's names and the word "beware". This shows that the author felt this paragraph was important and particularly wanted the reader to remember it.

Significance:

The word "want" is used to mean "in need" in this context. This quote is a comment on the greatest evils of mankind - suggesting that the ignorance of the rich creates such need in the poor and that both are ugly and unpleasant.

Related quotes:

"'Spirit are they yours?' Scrooge could say no more.
'They are Man's'"

Bigger picture:

This quote relates to the themes of *poverty* and *socialism vs capitalism*.

It carries a *moral message* to the reader and implies that people like Scrooge lie at the heart of the problem. However the use of the all-encompassing term "Man" - meaning mankind, also tells us that all people have some blame in the existence of these two children and their desperate state.

Use this quote in questions about:

Socialism vs capitalism
The Ghost of Christmas Present
Poverty and greed

Quote 60

"'Have they no refuge or resource?' cried Scrooge.
'Are there no Prisons?' said the Spirit, turning on him for the last time with his own words."

Techniques:

There is a *literary echo* here in Scrooge's own words being used against him again to highlight his misdemeanours.

Alliteration is used in "refuge or resource" to draw the reader's attention to the hypocrisy of Scrooge's question in the light of his earlier actions.

The Spirit uses a *rhetorical question* to remind Scrooge of his own words. This makes the reader think about the full impact of his earlier statements - which he did not think unreasonable at the time.

Significance:

This is the last spirit to actually speak to Scrooge, and indeed the last words any Spirit actually says to him, as the third Spirit does not speak at all. The impact of the last words being Scrooge's own words turned back on him is to leave him thinking about the cruelty and heartlessness of his own attitude before the Spirits' visits.

Bigger picture:

There is a sharp contrast here with Scrooge's previous statements that the poor should make use of prisons and him asking about refuge and resource for children who are clearly in need. We see that his character arc is almost complete, in that he is now actively asking how he can help those in need.

The quote relates to the themes of *poverty* and *socialism vs capitalism*.

Use this quote in questions about:

Socialism vs capitalism
The Ghost of Christmas Present
Poverty
Greed
Charity and generosity

Chapter 4 – A Christmas Carol Stave 4

Quote 61

"The phantom slowly, gravely, silently approached him"

Techniques:

Through the use of the word "grave" this *foreshadows* the subject of the spirit's visit. The *connotation* is that this spirit is Death himself.

A *list* of *adverbs* is used to create an eerie atmosphere and make the reader fear this final spirit.

Significance:

This final spirit does not speak, which adds to the fear it inspires in Scrooge. This is the only spirit to be described as a Phantom, which suggests it is somehow different to the other spirits and more terrifying. This Spirit did not wait for Scrooge to be back in bed before approaching but appeared as soon as its predecessor vanished.

Related quote:

"In the very air through which this Spirit moved it seemed to scatter gloom and mystery."

"A solemn phantom, draped and hooded, coming like a mist along the ground towards him." - this *simile* makes the spirit seem otherworldly.

Bigger Picture:

This quote relates to the theme of *death*. The uncertain appearance of the final Spirit also mirrors that the future is uncertain and can be altered based upon a person consciously choosing to change their life path.

Use this quote in questions about:

Death
The Ghost of Christmas Yet to Come
The spirit world

Quote 62

"It was shrouded in a deep black garment, which concealed its head, its face, its form."

Techniques:

A *list* of the parts concealed by the Spirit's cloak draws attention to how little of the spirit is revealed to Scrooge.

The colour black has the *connotation* of death.

Significance:

This spirit is not one that is meant to be known intimately by Scrooge as he has been able to know the other two spirits. This hints at the fact that Scrooge has the ability to change the future by changing his actions. He is in the presence of a spirit who may be death himself, and who has come to show Scrooge his own death. This is a fact the spirit does not reveal to him during the visit, not until the very end, and concealment is a strong theme for this Spirit.

Related quotes:

"It would have been difficult to detach the figure from the night and separate it from the darkness"

"He knew no more, for the Spirit neither spoke nor moved."

Bigger picture:

This quote relates to the theme of *death* and illustrates the terror of the Spirit world as well as that it is usually well concealed from human eyes.

Use this quote in questions about:

Death
The Ghost of Christmas Yet to Come
The spirit world

Quote 63

"As I hope to live to be another man from what I was, I am prepared to bear you company, and do it with a thankful heart."

Techniques:

The use of the *adjective* "thankful" shows that Scrooge is pleased to have the spirits visiting him and has absorbed their message.

The use of the *verb* "prepared" shows Scrooge's fear, and also bravery in facing that fear in order to change his ways.

Significance:

This is Scrooge's first declaration of absolute intent to change his ways. The reader is left in no doubt that the events of the Spirit's visits have altered him beyond recognition. Now that the reader has some sympathy with the changed Scrooge they are borne along on his fear throughout this encounter.

Related quotes:

"I fear you more than any spectre I have seen."

"Scrooge feared the silent shape so much that his legs trembled beneath him"

"Lead on! The night is waning fast and it is precious time to me, I know."

Bigger picture:

This quote relates to the theme of *redemption* and shows the extent of Scrooge's journey from miserly old man to compassionate person.

Use this quote in questions about:

Redemption
The Ghost of Christmas Yet to Come
The spirit world
Scrooge

Quote 64

"'It's likely to be a very cheap funeral,' said the same speaker, 'for, upon my life, I don't know of anybody to go it'"

Techniques:

This *dialogue* shows the lack of feeling the speaker had for Scrooge, and lack of sympathy even though he is dead. The use of the *adjective* "cheap" is related to the fact that Scrooge used to prize money above all else.

There is a *literary echo* here of how poorly attended Jacob Marley's funeral was.

Significance:

This quote shows that if Scrooge was to continue in the way he had been going before the Spirits' visits he would have died alone. If he was the "sole mourner" at Marley's funeral then there is nobody left at all to go to his. It illustrates a life lived lonely and miserable.

Related quotes:

"Scrooge was his sole executer, his sole administrator, his sole assign, his sole residuary legatee, his sole friend and sole mourner."

"What has he done with his money?" - shows the only thing people were concerned about for Mr Scrooge was the fortune he had amassed in his lonely life.

Bigger picture:

This quote relates to the themes of *death* and *redemption* it shows what Scrooge must change to avoid.

Use this quote in questions about:

Redemption
The Ghost of Christmas Yet to Come
The spirit world
Scrooge
Death

Quote 65

"Old Scratch has got his own at last, hey?"

Techniques:

A *rhetorical question* is used to add levity to the exchange. This shows that Scrooge's death was a matter of interest but not sorrow to these men.

The *colloquial phrase* "got his own" shows that these men were on friendly terms and the meeting was informal.

Significance:

This is another exchange that shows the lack of sorrow or emotion, other than vague interest, generated by Scrooge's death. A first-time reader would be curious as to who is dead, although may guess that the Spirit would be showing Scrooge his own future as the previous Spirits have shown him aspects of his own past and present.

Related quote:

"He had made a point always of standing well in their esteem" - shows that even those Scrooge had taken particular care to be nice to on account of their wealth and importance had little good to say about him.

Bigger Picture:

This quote is a *moral message* for the reader that those who are treated well by a person will still notice that he treats others badly and their esteem will be altered accordingly.

Use this quote in questions about:

Redemption
Scrooge
Death
Greed

Quote 66

"He resolved to treasure up every word he heard and everything he saw."

Techniques:

The *repetition* of the word "every" shows that this is an important facet of this quote, drawing the reader's attention to Scrooge's particular regard for the messages the Spirit is trying to give him.

The *verb* "resolved" suggests determination, in this case Scrooge's determination to learn from what he is shown by the spirits

Significance:

This shows Scrooge's change in character clearly. He has decided that whatever the Spirit has to show him he will take heed and will try to learn what he can from it. He is willing to listen, and that is very different to the man he was at the start of the night.

Related quotes:

"Feeling assured that they must have some hidden purpose, he set himself to consider what it was likely to be.

"He had an expectation that the conduct of his future self would give him the clue he missed."

Bigger picture:

This quote relates to the theme of *redemption*. It shows that Scrooge is determined to set himself on the path towards it.

Use this quote in questions about:

Redemption
Scrooge
Death

Quote 67

"She was closely followed by a man in faded black, who was no less startled to see them than they had been upon the recognition of each other."

Techniques:

The *verb* "startled" has *connotations* that suggest fright, as though they are aware that they might be caught doing something bad.

Significance:

This is the introduction of the three people who have taken items from Scrooge's death chamber. They are at first worried on seeing each other in case they have been found out in their wrong doing. After they recognise each other they begin to laugh, as they each know that there is little likelihood of anyone having any loyalty to Scrooge after all.

Related quotes:

"Look here, old Joe, here's a chance! If we haven't all three met here without meaning it!"

"They all three burst into a laugh"

Bigger picture:

This quote relates to the themes of *loneliness* and *poverty*. Scrooge is so alone that nobody cared enough to make sure his things were not stolen and those who worked for him so poor that they felt entitled to take a few items from his house.

Use this quote in questions about:

Loneliness
Poverty
Scrooge
Death

Quote 68

"Every person has a right to take care of themself. He always did!"

Who said it?
Mrs Dilber the charwoman.

Techniques:

An *exclamation* is used to add drama and power to the statement. Similarly the *short sentences* give a *tone* to the quote that suggests the statement cannot be argued with.

There is a *literary echo* here of Scrooge saying he should be left to mind his own business.

Significance:

This is the motto that Scrooge lived by, and his staff have used this as an excuse to justify stealing from him once he was dead. They would have known they could not have expected to get anything in the will and would need to have some means of supporting themselves with the work they used to do for Scrooge gone with him. They believe their actions to be justifiable.

Related quote:

"Who's the worse for the loss of a few things like these Not a dead man I suppose?"

Bigger picture:

This quote relates to the themes of *poverty* and *socialism vs capitalism*. It is a direct comment on the fact that Scrooge should have taken better care of those who worked for him.

Use this quote in questions about:

Loneliness
Poverty
Scrooge
Socialism vs capitalism

Quote 69

"Why wasn't he natural in his lifetime? If he had been he'd have had somebody to look after him when he was struck with death, instead of lying gasping out his last there alone, by himself."

Who said it?
The Laundress

Techniques:

A *rhetorical question* is used by Mrs Dilber as a persuasive technique to get old Joe to think the same way she did.

The *repetition* of the idea of aloneness emphasises that nobody was there to help the dead man in his final days.

Significance:

This quote has a defensive tone, and shows that the woman feels justified in her stealing because of who she has stolen from. It is possible she would have found similar excuses for stealing from anyone well off, but it is easier for her to justify stealing from a man who drive everyone away from him and made his own misery.

Related quote:

"It's the truest word was ever spoke,' said Mrs Dilber, 'It's a judgment on him'"

Bigger Picture:

This quote relates to the theme of *family* because it shows Scrooge had none in his last days, and to the theme of *redemption* as this is the fate he will be trying to avoid by mending his ways.

Use this quote in questions about:

Loneliness
Poverty
Scrooge
Socialism vs capitalism

Quote 70

"He viewed them with a detestation and disgust that could hardly have been greater, though they had been obscene demons, marketing the corpse itself."

Techniques:

A *semantic field* of unpleasantness and obscenity highlights how loathsome the scene was, watching people sell off items stolen from a dead man and talking about him as if he was not even human.

The *comparative* "greater" gives the reader a frame of reference by comparing to something that they would be able to picture easily.

Significance:

Scrooge is now seen looking at people who are taking advantage of a man's death as doing a terrible thing. He is disgusted by something that he himself would have been likely to do prior to the Spirits' visits. Scrooge has now realised that this is not a good way to live.

Related quotes:

"He was an excellent man of business on the very day of the funeral and solemnised it with an undoubted bargain."

"Scrooge listened to this dialogue in horror."

Bigger Picture:

This quote relates to the themes of *greed* and *socialism vs capitalism* as it shows that Scrooge has realised that profit is not the most important thing in life.

Use this quote in questions about:

Greed
Redemption
Scrooge
Socialism vs capitalism

Quote 71

"On it, plundered and bereft, unwatched, unwept and uncared for, was the body of this man."

Techniques:

A *list* is used with *alliteration* for added emphasis. The combining of these two techniques signals to the reader how important this image is.

The *verb* plundered reminds the reader that those who worked for Scrooge have taken everything they could from him and that he largely brought this state of affairs on himself.

Significance:

Scrooge does not know it but he is looking at his own dead body. The grief he thinks he feels that the passing of a stranger goes unmourned is actually grief for himself. This image provides him with even more motivation to mend his ways.

Related quotes:

"He frightened everyone away from him when he was alive, to profit us when he was dead."

"Beneath a ragged sheet there lay a something covered up."

Bigger picture:

This quote relates to the theme of *family* because it shows Scrooge had none, to the theme of *greed* because it shows the consequences of his greed when he was alive extending after his death.

It carries a *moral message* to the reader to be sure not to alienate people in life or they too will end up alone and unloved.

Use this quote in questions about:

Family
Greed
Scrooge

Quote 72

"Oh cold, cold, rigid dreadful Death, set up thine alter here, and dress it with such terrors as thou hast at thy command: for this is thy dominion! But of the loved, revered and honoured head thou canst not turn one hair to thy dread purposes, or make one feature odious."

Techniques:

The word "cold" is *repeated* for emphasis.

A *list of adjectives* with a *semantic field* of beloved creates a *contrast* with the list of *adjectives* meaning the opposite describing the body Scrooge sees lying before him in the previous paragraphs.

Significance:

This passage is an *aside* warning that Death and the Devil (who are portrayed as one by the use of the words "alter" and "terrors") take root where there is no love so a person who drives everyone away from them will be taken by the Devil after death, whilst a loved person who is righteous in his lifetime will be spared.

Related quotes:

"He can't look uglier than he did in that one."

"Strike, Shadow, Strike, and see his good deeds springing from the wound."

Bigger picture:

This quote relates to the themes of *death* and *family*. It implies that a person with the love of a family cannot be turned to the Devil's purposes.

Use this quote in questions about:

Family
Death
Scrooge
Loneliness

Quote 73

"She hurried to the door and met her husband; a man whose face was careworn and depressed, though he was young."

Techniques:

Imagery is used here to paint a vivid portrait of the husband and help the reader understand his state of mind.

A *semantic field* of unhappiness is used to describe how the young man looks and give the impression that he is under great stress.

Significance:

This couple owed money to Scrooge, and he was not an understanding man so the husband is stressed at trying to find the loan repayments so that the family are not thrown out on the street. This shows the extent of the misery Scrooge inflicted on others as well as on himself.

Related quotes:

"She was expecting someone, and with anxious eagerness."

"If there is any person in this town who feels emotion caused by this man's death," said Scrooge, quite agonised, "show that person to me, Spirit! I beseech you!"

Bigger picture:

This quote relates to the themes of *poverty* and *socialism vs capitalism*.

Use this quote in questions about:

Poverty
Socialism vs capitalism
Scrooge
Family
Greed
Redemption

Quote 74

"'He is past relenting,' said her husband, 'he is dead.' ... She was thankful in her soul to hear it."

Techniques:

Short sentences add drama to the declaration made in this *dialogue*.

The *verb* "relenting" suggests that someone has power over them and could use that power to help them but is refusing to do so.

Significance:

This is the emotion the Spirit has shown Scrooge. Not a single person in the town feels any sorrow for the dead man, but this couple had their lives so ruined by him that they are pleased and relieved to hear that he has died. This shocking fact illustrates the extent to which the dead man was hated and resented.

Related quote:

"She prayed forgiveness the next moment and was sorry; but the first was the emotion of her heart."

"It would be bad fortune indeed to find so merciless a creditor in his successor. We may sleep tonight with light heats, Caroline!"

Bigger picture:

This quote relates to the themes of *poverty* and *socialism vs capitalism*. It is also a moral message to the reader not to allow themselves to be too harsh with people they might feel owe them something in case they too reach a point where people are relieved to see them gone.

Use this quote in questions about:

Poverty
Socialism vs capitalism
Scrooge
Greed
Redemption

Quote 75

"'He was very light to carry,' she resumed, 'and his father loved him so, that it was no trouble: no trouble.'"

Who said it?
Mrs Cratchitt.

Techniques:

The *repetition* of the words "no trouble" emphasise the idea that a person who is loved is no burden on the people around them, and the distress of Mrs Cratchitt at Tiny Tim's passing.

The reaction of the Cratchit's to Tiny Tim's death is a *contrast* to the reactions of those who knew Scrooge to his death.

Significance:

Tiny Tim has passed away and the Cratchitt's are in mourning. Mrs Cratchitt is expressing how loved he was, and how the family misses him. Saying he was "light to carry" has two meanings, the literal meaning that he did not weigh very much for his father to carry on his shoulders, and the deeper meaning that his presence was such a light burden on the family that it was almost no trouble at all to have him there. The Spirit is showing Scrooge that people are mourning the child he had the power to help but did not far more than they are mourning him.

Related quotes:

"I think he has walked a little slower than he used, these last few evenings."

Bigger picture:

This quote relates to the theme of *family*.

Use this quote in questions about:

Family
Death
The Cratchitt family
Tiny Tim

Quote 76

"'It wasn't,' cried Bob, 'for the sake of anything he might be able to do for us, so much as for his kind way, that this was quite delightful.'"

Who said it?
Bob Cratchitt - about Scrooge's nephew.

Techniques:

There is a *semantic field* of niceness seen here, which shows that Scrooge's nephew was a pleasant person to encounter.

Significance:

This quote shows that it was not the offer of money or help that made Bob Cratchitt so pleased to see Fred, but only his kindness. It shows that a person does not have to be rich, or spend a great deal of money, to be able to make the lives of others a little better. It also shows that Fred remained kind and pleasant throughout the years, and became beloved by those around him, even though Scrooge continued to be miserly and unpleasant.

Related quote:

"'I'm sure he's a good soul,' said Mrs Cratchitt.
'You would be sure of it my dear," returned Bob, 'If you saw and spoke to him."

Bigger picture:

This quote relates to the themes of *kindness* and *generosity*.

Use this quote in questions about:

Kindness
Generosity
Fred
Charity
Poverty

Quote 77

"However and whenever we part from one another, I am sure we shall none of us forget Tiny Tim - shall we - or this first parting that was among us?"

Who said it?
Bob Cratchitt

Techniques:

The *repetition* of the word "part" draws attention to the fact that Tiny Tim has gone forever.

A *rhetorical question* is used to make the reader think more deeply about the impact Tiny Tim had on the Cratchitt family, and the story as a whole.

Significance:

This quote suggests that all families part in the end as children grow up and leave home, but that, even in death, families are bound together by the love in their souls, as none of them can forget each other.

Related quotes:

"We shall not quarrel among ourselves, and forget Tiny Tim in doing it."

"Spirit of Tiny Tim, thy childish essence was from God."

Bigger picture:

This quote relates to the themes of *family* and *love*.

Use this quote in questions about:

Family
The Cratchitt family
Tiny Tim
Death
Religion
Love

Quote 78

"Are these the shadows of the things that Will be, or are they shadows of things that May be only?"

Who said it?
Scrooge.

Techniques:

Scrooge *repeats* the word shadows in his *question* which indicates the things he has seen are changeable and impermanent.

The *capitalisation* mid-sentence of "Will" and "May" suggests a particular emphasis on those words as Scrooge is speaking and hints at the desperation in his *tone of voice*.

Significance:

Scrooge asks this immediately before looking at the name on the grave stone. This suggests that he is afraid of seeing his own name and wants to be assured that he can change his fate if he changes his ways.

Related quote:

"If the courses be departed from, the ends will change. Say it is thus with what you show me!"

"The Spirit was as immovable as ever."

Bigger picture:

This quote relates to the themes of *death* and *redemption*. It shows that Scrooge is desperate to know that it is not too late for him to achieve redemption.

Use this quote in questions about:

Death
Redemption
Scrooge
How the visits of the spirits affect Scrooge

Quote 79

"Scrooge crept towards it, trembling as he went; and, following the finger, read upon the neglected grave his own name."

Techniques:

The use of the *verbs* "Trembling" and "crept" show Scrooge's fear that the man on the bed might be himself.

The use of the *adjective* "neglected" shows that there was nobody to care for the grave any more than there was anybody to attend the funeral.

The *alliteration* in "following the finger" draws attention to this passage and creates tension before the reveal that the name on the grave is Scrooge's own.

Significance:

This quote confirms what the reader may have suspected - that Scrooge is the dead man for whom nobody cared. That Scrooge is now scared that this could be his fate shows that he is a changed man.

Related quote:

"'Am I that man who lay upon the bed?' he cried upon his knees."

Bigger picture:

This quote relates to the themes of *death* and *redemption*. It can also be linked with the theme of *family* as it is usually family members who tend a grave and Scrooge's grave was untended, indicating that if he had any family they did not care for him.

Use this quote in questions about:

Death
Redemption
Scrooge
How the visits of the spirits affect Scrooge
Family

Quote 80

"I am not the man I was. I will not be the man I must have been but for this intercourse. Why show me this, if I am past all hope?"

Techniques:

Scrooge pleads with the Spirit using a *rhetorical question* which makes the reader wonder about the answer to the question.

The *repetition* of the idea that Scrooge is a changed man shows how seriously he is taking this process.

Significance:

Scrooge has every motivation now to change his ways and this quote shows his commitment to doing so. It shows his desperation to avoid the fate he has been shown by the Spirit.

Related quotes:

"I will honour Christmas in my heart, and try to keep it all the year."

"I will live in the Past, the Present and the Future. The Spirits of all Three shall strive within me." - this has a religious *connotation* in the triad of the father, the son and the holy ghost.

Bigger picture:

This quote relates to the theme of *redemption* as it shows Scrooge determined and desperate to be redeemed.

Use this quote in questions about:

Redemption
Scrooge
How the visits of the spirits affect Scrooge
Christmas

Chapter 5 – A Christmas Carol Stave 5

Quote 81

"Best and happiest of all, the time before him was his own, to make amends in!"

Techniques:

A *semantic field* suggesting positivity and happiness is used here to show Scrooge's relief at the visits being over.

An *exclamation* is used to bring urgency and excitement to the passage.

Significance:

This quote shows that even when the spirits have gone Scrooge retains his desire to redeem himself and is truly a changed man. The positive tone at the start of this stave shows that it will be different to the other four staves. This is an indication to the reader that Scrooge is changed forever.

Related quotes:

"'I will live in the past, the present and the future,' Scrooge repeated as he scrambled out of bed."

"Yes! And the bedpost was his own."

"Oh tell me I may sponge away the writing on this stone!"

Bigger picture:

This quote relates to the themes of *redemption* and *happiness*. It shows the beginning of the contrast between the misery of the first four staves and the happy ending in this final stave.

Use this quote in questions about:

Redemption
Scrooge
How the visits of the spirits affect Scrooge
Happiness

Quote 82

"He was so fluttered and so glowing with his good intentions, that his broken voice would scarcely answer to his call."

Techniques:

There is a *positive tone* in the description of Scrooge in this quote through the use of the *adjectives* "fluttered" and "glowing".

There is a *literary echo* here in the use of the word "glowing" as this is how Fred was described in the first stave when he was introduced. This creates a *comparison* between Scrooge and his nephew.

Significance:

Describing Scrooge now in similar terms to those used to describe his nephew in the first stave shows the extent of his transformation. The reader was primed to like Fred, who is good and kind, and therefore is now being asked to like Scrooge, who it is implied is now as worthy of admiration as his nephew.

Related quotes:

"He was all in a glow; his face was ruddy and handsome; his eyes sparkled, and his breath smoked again."

"For he is the pleasantest-spoken gentleman you ever heard."

(both quotes said of Fred in stave 1 and stave 4 respectively.)

Bigger picture:

This quote relates to the theme of *redemption*.

Use this quote in questions about:

Redemption
Scrooge
How the visits of the spirits affect Scrooge
Fred
The author's idea of a "good man".

Quote 83

"I am as light as a feather, I am as happy as an angel, I am as merry as a school-boy. I am as giddy as a drunken man."

Who said it?
Scrooge.

Techniques:

A *list* of *similes* is used to show Scrooge's high spirits using *comparisons* to things that the reader can easily relate to.

A *semantic field* suggesting high spirits is found within this quote.

Significance:

This shows the change in Scrooge to its fullest. He was previously so miserable he did not smile and was unhappy all the time. Now he is happy to be alive and relieved to have an opportunity to change his ways for the better.

Related quotes:

"'I don't know what to do!' cried Scrooge. laughing and crying in the same breath."

"No wind that blew was bitterer than he." (shows *contrast* with his previous self.)

Bigger picture:

This quote relates to the themes of *happiness* and *redemption*.

Use this quote in questions about:

Redemption
Happiness
Scrooge
How the visits of the spirits affect Scrooge

Quote 84

"He was checked in his transports by the churches ringing out the lustiest peals he had ever heard. Clash, clash, hammer, ding, dong, bell! Bell, dong, ding; hammer, clang, clash."

Techniques:

Onomatopoeia is used to help the reader to clearly imagine the scene using all of their senses.

A *superlative* is used ("lustiest") to give the statement power and establish that this is a time of new and better things.

A long *list* of sounds is used to suggest the bells will go on ringing forever.

Significance:

These are the same church bells Scrooge has been hearing for many years, yet today he able to appreciate them more because he is in such a good mood and has decided to change. This illustrates how much Scrooge has changed as he would not previously have taken any notice of the bells.

Bigger picture:

This quote relates to the theme of *happiness*. It also suggests that by renewing its effort to be pleasant the outside world is joining in Scrooge's good mood.

Use this quote in questions about:

Redemption
Happiness
Scrooge
How the visits of the spirits affect Scrooge
Christmas

Quote 85

"I haven't missed it. The Spirits have done it all in one night. They can do anything they like. Of course they can. Of course they can."

Who said it?
Scrooge

Techniques:

Short sentences make this scene appear more dramatic and exciting, building anticipation of what could happen next.

Repetition of the phrase "Of course they can" suggests Scrooge would have been naive to think otherwise.

Significance:

Scrooge has not missed Christmas day and can begin to make amends immediately. There is a certain satisfaction for the reader in thinking that his first day as a changed man will be Christmas day and he will be able to make this Christmas a merry one to set an example for the rest of the year.

Related quotes:

"'I don't know what day of the month it is,' said Scrooge 'I don't know how long I have been among the spirits. I don't know anything.'"

Bigger Picture:

This quote relates to the themes of *Christmas* as Scrooge is delighted he has not missed it, and *redemption,* as it is symbolic that it is Christmas day on which Scrooge should begin seeking redemption.

Use this quote in questions about:

Redemption
Happiness
Scrooge
Christmas
The world of spirits

Quote 86

"'I shall send it to Bob Cratchitt's,' whispered Scrooge, rubbing his hands and splitting with a laugh."

Techniques:

The use of the *verb* "whispered" suggests an air of confidentiality in the action.

The *tone* of the quote is celebratory and positive.

Significance:

This is the first action Scrooge takes to begin his path to redemption. It is fitting that the first person he thinks of should be his poor clerk as it is Bob whose life has been made the most miserable by Scrooge in recent years through the fact that he has spent the most time with him. It was also Tiny Tim that pulled at Scrooge's heart strings in the visits from the spirits and therefore it is natural that he should think first of him.

Related quotes:

"He shan't know who sends it. It's twice the size of Tiny Tim."

"The hand in which he wrote the address was not a steady one; but write it he did, somehow."

Bigger picture:

This quote relates to the themes of *Christmas, generosity* and *redemption.*

Use this quote in questions about:

Redemption
Happiness
Scrooge
Christmas
Generosity and charity

Quote 87

"The chuckle with which he paid for the turkey, and the chuckle with which he paid for the cab, and the chuckle with which he recompensed the boy, were only to be exceeded by the chuckle with which he sat down breathless in the chair again."

Techniques:

The *repetition* of the *noun* "chuckle" creates a light hearted atmosphere and emphasises how happy Scrooge was at his act of charity.

The references to paying for things *imply* that Scrooge has changed in his attitude to spending money.

Significance:

Scrooge is laughing and this is something he has not previously done a lot of. That so much emphasis is being placed on his laughter, and the fact that he is paying for things to benefit other people is a clear indication to the reader that this is not the same man they were first introduced to at the beginning of the book. He has entirely transformed.

Related quotes:

"For a man who had been out of practice for so many years it was a splendid laugh, a most illustrious laugh."

Bigger Picture:

This quote is related to Scrooge's character arc, in that it illustrates the extent of his transformation.

It is related to the themes of *happiness, generosity* and *redemption*.

Use this quote in questions about:

Redemption
Happiness
Scrooge and the effect of the spirits on Scrooge
Generosity
Greed and attitudes to money

Quote 88

"He looked so irresistibly pleasant, in a word, that three or four good humoured fellows said, 'Good morning sir! A merry Christmas to you!'"

Techniques:

This quote creates a *contrast* with the way Scrooge was described at the beginning of the book. There is a *semantic field* of pleasantness seen here to create a positive and happy *tone*.

The use of the *adverb* "irresistibly" suggests that Scrooge now draws people to him rather than pushing them away.

Significance:

Scrooge has previously cultivated an aura of unpleasantness and discouraged people from speaking to him. In this quote we see the full extent of the change that has come upon him overnight as other people are now swept up in his good mood and no longer afraid to wish him a merry Christmas.

Related quotes:

"Scrooge said often afterwards that, of all the blithe sounds he had ever heard, those were the blithest in his ears."

"Nobody ever stopped him in the street to say, with gladsome looks, 'My dear Scrooge how are you?'"

Bigger Picture.

This quote relates to the themes of *redemption, Christmas* and *socialism vs capitalism* it shows a contrast between how negatively Scrooge was described as a capitalist and how positively he is described as a socialist.

Use this quote in questions about:

Scrooge and the effect of the spirits on Scrooge
Socialism vs Capitalism
Redemption

Quote 89

"Not a farthing less. A great many back payments are included in it, I assure you. Will you do me that favour?"

Who said it?
Scrooge to the man from the charity who had been collecting for the poor the previous day.

Techniques:

A **rhetorical question** is used to persuade that Scrooge is serious in his proposition.

Significance:

Scrooge is pleased to have seen the man from the charity as he can now make amends for his poor actions the day before. In saying that he believes "back payments" are owed he shows that he realises he should have been helping those less fortunate all along.

Related quotes:

"I help to support the establishments I have mentioned - they cost enough; and those who are badly off must go there." (Scrooge regarding prisons, workhouses etc. paid for through his taxes.)

Bigger picture:

This quote relates to the themes of *generosity* and *redemption*.

Use this quote in questions about:

Scrooge and the effect of the spirits on Scrooge
Socialism vs capitalism
Redemption
Generosity
Charity

Quote 90

"He ... patted children on the head, and questioned beggars, and looked down into the kitchens of houses, and up to the windows; and found that everything could yield him pleasure."

Techniques:

A *list* of items Scrooge found interesting is used to build excitement and sweep the reader along in Scrooge's emotion.

There is a *literary echo* from the first stave when the list of people who ignored him on the street included children and beggars.

Significance:

Scrooge was previously so miserable nobody would communicate with him - beggars would not even rattle their cups at him. The contrast between that state and the one described here is dramatic. It would be impossible to tell that the two descriptions were of the same man if someone took the two passages out of context.

Related quotes:

"He had never dreamed that any walk - that anything - could give him so much happiness."

"No beggars implored him to bestow a trifle, no children asked him what it was O'clock."

Bigger picture:

This quote relates to the themes of *happiness* and *redemption*.

Use this quote in questions about:

Scrooge and the effect of the spirits on Scrooge
Redemption
Happiness
Socialism vs capitalism

Quote 91

"He passed the door a dozen times before he had the courage to go up and knock. But he made a dash and did it."

Techniques:

A *short sentence* is used to give dramatic impact to Scrooge's accomplishing the feat of knocking on the door.

The use of the *verb* "dash" implies that Scrooge had to knock quickly or he might have lost his nerve and the *alliteration* in "door a dozen" draws attention to Scrooge's hesitation.

Significance:

Although Scrooge was previously invited to his nephew's home for dinner he is still unsure of his welcome. He is aware that he has behaved badly towards Fred and is nervous in case he is too late to make amends and is sent away. This shows he feels remorse for the way he acted in being so unkind to his nephew.

Related quotes:

"He turned it gently and sidled his face in around the door," - shows hesitation and nervousness.

"What right have you to be merry? You're poor enough?" - an unkind comment made to Fred that is an example of the previous actions that have made Scrooge so nervous

Bigger Picture:

This quote relates to the themes of *family* and *redemption,* because he is going to make amends with his nephew.

Use this quote in questions about:

Scrooge and the effect of the spirits on Scrooge
Redemption
Family

Quote 92

"Let him in! It is a mercy he didn't shake his arm off. He was at home in five minutes. Nothing could be heartier."

Techniques:

An *exclamation* and *short sentences* are used to create an excited atmosphere in this quote.

A *comparative* is used in "heartier" to emphasise how pleasant the atmosphere was.

hyperbole is used in describing the shaking of the arm and how quickly Scrooge felt at home to show Fred's good and forgiving nature, and emphasise the excitement of the moment.

Significance:

Scrooge is accepted at once by his nephew and welcomed as though he had never said a mean word to him in his life. This shows that people from Scrooge's past that he has treated badly are willing to forgive him. This suggests to the reader that Scrooge can achieve redemption if he continues with his new attitude.

Related quotes:

"It's I. Your uncle Scrooge. I have come to dinner. Will you let me in Fred?"

Bigger picture:

This quote relates to the themes of *family* and *redemption*.

Use this quote in questions about:

Scrooge and the effect of the spirits on Scrooge
Redemption
Family
Fred

Quote 93

"Wonderful party, wonderful games, wonderful unanimity, won-der-ful happiness."

Techniques:

The *list* of wonderful things and *repetition* of the word wonderful itself emphasises how happy everyone was on Christmas day.

The unorthodox use of the *hyphens* in the last "won-der-ful" changes how the reader pronounces the word in their heads and makes it memorable.

Significance:

This is a moment that Scrooge saw in the visit from the second Spirit but had not experienced himself since his time with Fezziwig. It shows he is joining in with the Christmas day celebrations with the true spirit of Christmas.

Related quotes:

"The consequence of him taking a dislike to us and not making merry with us is, as I think, that he loses some pleasant moments which could do him no harm."

"After a while they played at forfeits, for it is good to be children sometimes and never better than at Christmas,"

Bigger picture:

This quote relates to the themes of *family* and *happiness* and *Christmas*.

Use this quote in questions about:

Scrooge and the effect of the spirits on Scrooge
Redemption
Family
Fred
Christmas
Happiness

Quote 94

"If only he could be there early and catch Bob Cratchitt coming late! That was the thing he had set his heart upon."

Techniques:

An *exclamation* is used to add excitement to the sentence.

The use of the *noun* "heart" has *connotations* that this action is being taken out of love, and not out of spite as it would once have been.

Significance:

Scrooge has already improved the Cratchitt's Christmas by sending the enormous turkey to them for Christmas dinner, and now wishes to surprise Bob Cratchitt. First though he intends to play a little joke, so that Bob is all the happier when his true surprise is revealed.

Related quotes:

"You'll keep your Christmas by losing your situation."

"Be here all the earlier next morning."

"What do you mean by coming here at this time of day?"

Bigger picture:

This quote relates to the themes of *generosity* and *redemption*.

Use this quote in questions about:

Bob Cratchitt
Generosity
Scrooge and how he has changed
Christmas
Redemption

Quote 95

"The clock struck nine. No Bob. A quarter past. No Bob."

Techniques:

The *repetition* of the phrase "no Bob" builds anticipation.

The use of *short sentences* adds drama and excitement to this passage.

Significance:

The reader at this point is desperate to know what will happen when Bob Cratchitt finally turns up for work. He is going to get a great surprise, and the author is dragging out his arrival to maximum effect. This mirrors the excitement Scrooge is feeling at being able to deliver the good news to Bob and show him that his boss is a changed man.

Related quotes:

"He was on his stool in a jiffy; driving with his pen as if he were trying to overtake 9 o'clock" - This *simile* helps us to see how anxious Bob is at being late.

Bigger picture:

This quote is part of Scrooge's character arc. To see him excited to deliver a surprise rather than angry that his time is being wasted shows how far his character has come.

Use this quote in questions about:

Bob Cratchitt
Generosity
Scrooge and how he has changed
Christmas
Redemption

Quote 96

"I am not going to stand this sort of thing any longer. And therefore ... I am about to raise your salary."

Techniques:

This *dialogue* includes a surprise for Bob Cratchitt, and finally reveals to the reader what Scrooge means to do in catching him coming late to work.

Significance:

Scrooge is pretending at first to be his old self to play a joke on Bob. Indeed he is so unlike himself when he offers to raise the man's salary that Bob is startled, and doesn't know whether to take him seriously. This is the last thing Scrooge needs to rectify in his life - the way he treats his employees - having already fixed his uncharitable ways and mended fences with his remaining family.

Related quotes:

"My clerk with 15 shillings a week," shows that even Scrooge knows how poorly his clerk is paid.

"The founder of the feast indeed!" cried Mrs Cratchitt, reddening.

"He had a momentary idea of knocking Scrooge down with it, holding him and calling to the people in the court for help and a strait-waistcoat." - Bob fears that Scrooge has gone mad, and does not believe he would ever actually raise his salary.

Bigger picture:

This quote relates to the themes of *generosity* and *redemption*.

Use this quote in questions about:

Bob Cratchitt
Generosity
Scrooge and how he has changed
Redemption

Quote 97

"A merrier Christmas Bob, my good fellow, than I have given you for many a year! I'll raise your salary, and endeavour to assist your struggling family, and we'll discuss your affairs this very afternoon."

Techniques:

The *comparative* "merrier" is used to show that this is a change in how things are done.

A *list* of things he is going to do to make Bob's life better indicates Scrooge has thought about this at some length, and reinforces for the reader how important making amends with Bob is for Scrooge's redemption.

Significance:

Scrooge's transformation is complete. He wishes to help Bob's family and means to do a proper job if it. Scrooge is motivated partly by his concern for Tiny Tim, for whom he was most distressed during the Spirits' visits. This quote shows he is recognising his previous wrongdoing and wishes to make amends for that.

Related quote:

"'A merry Christmas Bob!' Said Scrooge with an earnestness that could not be mistaken."

Bigger picture:

This quote relates to the themes of *redemption, generosity,* and *Christmas.*

Use this quote in questions about:

Bob Cratchitt
Generosity
Scrooge and how he has changed
Redemption
Christmas

Quote 98

"Make up the fires and buy another coal-scuttle before you dot another i, Bob Cratchitt!"

Who said it?
Scrooge

Techniques:

An *exclamation* is used to show Scrooge's excitement.

Significance:

Scrooge previously would not allow Bob to have much of a fire at all to keep him warm without threatening to fire him. That he is now instructing him to make fires and buy more coal, despite the fact that the coal will cost money, shows the extent to which Scrooge has changed, and that he now knows the value of people to be greater than the value of money.

Related quotes:

"The clerk's fire was so very much smaller that it looked like one coal."

"The clerk put on his white comforter and tried to warm himself at the candle."

Bigger picture:

This quote relates to the themes of *redemption,* and *generosity.*

Use this quote in questions about:

Money
Generosity
Scrooge and how he has changed
Redemption

Quote 99

"He became as good a friend, as good a master, and as good a man as the good old city knew."

Techniques:

The *repetition* of the word "good" shows the reader that it is important to remember that Scrooge became a good man in the end.

The city of London is *personified* in "good old city knew" to give an impression that everyone now knew that Scrooge had become a good man.

Significance:

The author has completely changed the language used to describe Scrooge in this final stave, and this quote is the pinnacle of that. Scrooge would not have been described as good by any person prior to the Spirits' visits. This reinforces that he is a completely changed man. The inclusion of the word "friend" is telling, as previously Scrooge had no friends. He was barely on speaking terms with his own nephew and spoke civilly only to other wealthy men who made good business contacts.

Related quotes:

"I'm not at all sure I wasn't his most particular friend; for we used to stop and speak whenever we met."

"He had made a point always of standing well in their esteem: in a business point of view, that it; strictly in a business point of view."

Bigger picture:

This quote relates to the theme of *redemption* and shows that Scrooge achieved this redemption through completely changing his ways.

Use this quote in questions about:

Scrooge and how he has changed
Redemption
The author's idea of a "good man"

Quote 100

"It was always said of him that he knew how to keep Christmas well, if any man alive possessed the knowledge.

Techniques:

This is a *chiasmus* where the second part of the phrase is an approximated reversal of the first, used to emphasise a point and make it more memorable.

The use of the word "always" is an *exaggeration* or even *hyperbole*.

Significance:

This is the final statement made about Scrooge in the book. It shows that his previous attitude to Christmas has changed completely. This reflects that his entire character has changed completely.

Related quotes:

"Bah! Humbug!" - Scrooge's previous response to the mention of Christmas.

"But you don't keep it!" - Fred said this to Scrooge in Stave one, showing how little value Scrooge placed upon Christmas at that time.

Bigger picture:

It is of course not Christmas itself that was the important thing to Scrooge's redemption but what Christmas represents; namely a time for getting together and enjoying the companionship of friends and family. The spirit of Christmas is to be more generous, more helpful to other people, and more joyous than at other times of year
This quote relates to the themes of *Christmas* and *redemption*.

Use this quote in questions about:

Scrooge and how he has changed
Redemption
Christmas

Last Word

I hope you find this little book useful and that it helps you with your exams.

If you have liked this book keep an eye out for more books in the 100 Key Quotes series. Please also tell your friends – the more popular these books are, the more time I will be able to devote to them and the faster I will be able to produce them!

Coming soon:

100 Key Quotes for English Literate Revision: An Inspector Calls

100 Key Quotes for English Literate Revision: Of Mice and Men

100 Key Quotes for English Literate Revision: Jekyll and Hyde

Good luck with your exams.

From

Sarah Hindmarsh and The Creating With Kohla Publications Team.

Printed in Great Britain
by Amazon